W9-DDJ-431

Going to Work ANIMAL EDITION · Going to Work ANIMAL EDITION · Going to Work ANIMAL EDITION · Going to Work
NIMAL EDITION · Going to Work ANIMAL EDITION · Going to Work ANIMAL EDITION · Going to Work ANIMAL EDIT
Going to Work ANIMAL EDITION · Going to Work ANIMAL EDITION · Going to Work ANIMAL EDITION · Going to Wo
NIMAL EDITION · Going to Work ANIMAL EDITION · Going to Work ANIMAL EDITION · Going to Work ANIMAL EDITI

Going To Work
ANIMAL EDITION

3 1526 03781028 7

WITHDRAWN

Crime-Fighting Animals

ABDO
Publishing Company

A Buddy **Book by**
Julie Murray

VISIT US AT
www.abdopublishing.com

Published by ABDO Publishing Company, 8000 West 78th Street, Edina, Minnesota 55439.

Copyright © 2009 by Abdo Consulting Group, Inc. International copyrights reserved in all countries. No part of this book may be reproduced in any form without written permission from the publisher. Buddy Books™ is a trademark and logo of ABDO Publishing Company.

Printed in the United States.

Coordinating Series Editor: Rochelle Baltzer
Editor: Sarah Tieck
Contributing Editor: Marcia Zappa
Graphic Design: Maria Hosley
Cover Photograph: *AP Photo:* Ed Andrieski
Interior Photographs/Illustrations: *AP Photo:* Joe Cavaretta (p. 30), Sergio Dionisio (p. 20), Caleb Jones (p. 7), Peter De Jong (p. 25), Tim Larsen (p. 23), Marty Lederhandler (p. 27), Alan Marler (p. 19), Suzy Powell/The Town Talk (p. 15), Nick Ut (p. 21), Paul Vathis (p. 5); *iStockPhoto:* emmanuelle bonzami (p. 13), Amy Walters (p. 10); *Library of Congress* (p. 9); *Photos.com:* Jupiter Images (pp. 11, 17, 29); *Shutterstock:* Kuznetsov Alexey Andreevich (p. 25), Dennis Donohue (p. 7).

Library of Congress Cataloging-in-Publication Data

Murray, Julie, 1969-
  Crime-fighting animals / Julie Murray.
    p. cm. -- (Going to work)
  ISBN 978-1-60453-561-7
  1. Animals in police work--Juvenile literature. 2. Police dogs--Juvenile literature. 3. Police horses--Juvenile literature. I. Title.

  HV8025.M95 2009
  363.2'32--dc22

                                                              2008044272

Contents

Animals At Work

Going to work is an important part of life. At work, people use their skills to accomplish tasks and earn money.

Animals can have jobs, too. Many times, they complete tasks that human workers can't.

Some animals fight crime. They guard people and find clues. This is worthwhile work.

Dogs are among the animals that fight crime. They work with different types of police.

Helping Out

Crime-fighting animals are specially trained workers. Dogs and horses are the most common of these animals.

Crime-fighting animals assist police officers and other law-enforcement officials. They search for clues, guard suspects, and help control crowds. They work at airports, crime scenes, and large events.

Crime-fighting animals help law-enforcement officials do a better job. Animals have natural skills that make them ideal for this type of work.

HISTORY LESSON

Animals have helped fight crime for many years. Police cars were not commonly used until the early 1900s. Before that, police officers rode horses. Horses moved fast over far **distances**. They sometimes pulled wagons carrying prisoners.

In 1899, the first police car was used in Akron, Ohio. It traveled 18 miles per hour (29 km/h)!

Did You Know?

Many years ago, lots of police officers had horses! Today, there are just a few horses on most police forces.

Today, some firehouses keep Dalmatians as mascots. Mascots represent groups, such as firefighters or sports teams.

Before the 1900s, Dalmatians worked as crime-fighting animals. Known as **carriage** dogs, they helped clear paths for horse-drawn fire carts. They also helped guard firehouses and fire tools.

The first known police dogs were trained in Belgium in the early 1900s. The dogs joined officers on night patrols.

Belgian officers often used sheepdogs for police work.

Working Together

Crime-fighting animals accompany police officers to crime scenes and on patrol. So, they are trained to obey. Dogs also work to become strong and fast.

After basic training, some animals train for special jobs. Dogs may learn to sniff out clues or guard people. Horses may learn to stay calm or jump while carrying a rider.

Police dogs may need to jump walls or climb stairs. So, dogs in training do practice drills to prepare.

Some dogs are trained in Europe for police work. They may learn commands in languages other than English. So, officers learn to give commands in the language the dog understands.

Did You Know?

Some crime-fighting animals wear special gear, such as **harnesses** and vests. These keep them safe and help people recognize them.

Crime-fighting animals must pay attention to their work. In public, people might try to touch or feed the animals. But, doing this interrupts important work.

Laws protect crime-fighting animals. In some states, people must treat them with the same respect as officers.

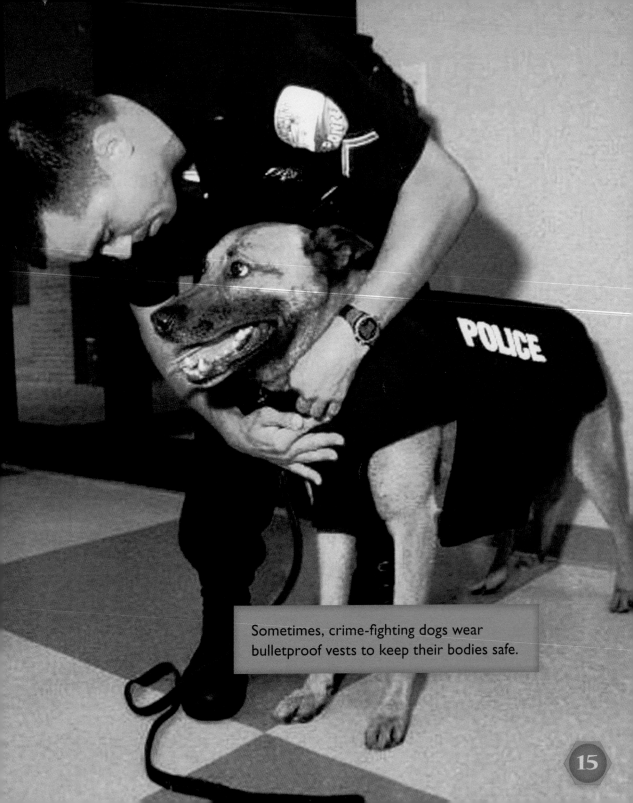

Sometimes, crime-fighting dogs wear bulletproof vests to keep their bodies safe.

Crime Fighters

Police dogs and officers are paired together. The dog's officer is called its handler. A police dog and its handler form a K-9 unit.

When a K-9 unit patrols, the dog helps find **suspects**. It guards them so they don't escape. It may bark to get its handler's attention. If a suspect tries to run away, the dog may bite or attack. This helps the police catch and arrest **criminals**.

Labrador retrievers (*top left*), German shepherds (*right*), and Belgian Malinois (*bottom left*) are common breeds used for police work.

Super Sniffers

Dogs are important crime fighters because of their **sensitive** noses. A dog's sense of smell is 50 times stronger than a human's! Also, dogs can separate smells. These natural skills save officers time during searches.

Dogs can sniff out unsafe people and objects. This helps keep officers from being surprised and hurt.

19

Police dogs and their handlers work together to find illegal items. This helps keep communities safe.

Some police dogs are specially trained to help police find illegal items. These items can include **drugs** and **bombs**. The dogs can find them hidden on someone's body, in buildings, or in other places.

In airports, police dogs sniff suitcases. They find items that are not allowed on aircraft. These items include weapons and certain foods.

Lost And Found

Tracking dogs help police find missing persons or objects. These dogs track, or follow, scents. This important job provides clues for police. Tracking dogs also help officers find **suspects** who are hiding.

Bloodhounds are known as tracking dogs.

Hoofed Helper

Sometimes police ride horses. This is called a mounted patrol. Mounted police ride through wilderness and city streets.

On horseback, an officer can see more of an area and move quickly. And because of the horse's size, people can see the officer better.

Police horses work in wilderness settings, such as beaches (*above*). They keep people safe in cities, too. Mounted patrols guard famous buildings, such as England's Buckingham Palace (*below*).

Did You Know?

The Royal Canadian Mounted Police are famous. The "Mounties" are known for their bright red coats and trusty horses. Today. Mounties only ride horses for special events.

Mounted patrols often help control crowds. They are used at concerts, parades, and other large events. On horseback, officers are better able to control large, excited crowds of people.

Horses make police officers more effective. One mounted officer is like having about ten officers on the ground.

Gifted Workers

Crime-fighting animals work to protect people. They help solve crimes and save lives. These animals do important work that makes the world a safer place!

Police officers and their dogs are together around the clock. They often form strong friendships.

The Animal Times

Honorary Helpers

Police dogs are very important. When they die, some are honored in the same way as police officers.

Comfort and Clues

Some dogs are trained to find dead bodies, or cadavers. They are called cadaver dogs. Finding a person's body can comfort a family. Also, it may give new clues to a crime.

Important Words

bomb (BAHM) a case filled with something that explodes when set off.

carriage (KEHR-ihj) a vehicle with wheels used for carrying people. It is often pulled by a horse.

criminal (KRIH-muh-nuhl) someone who has broken the law.

distance the length between two points.

drug something that affects the brain, causes addiction, and is often illegal.

enforcement (ihn-FAWR-smuhnt) the action of carrying out something, such as laws.

harness an arrangement of straps used to hold on to or attach something to an animal.

sensitive able to quickly and easily feel or notice.

suspect someone that officials believe may have broken the law.

Web Sites

To learn more about crime-fighting animals, visit ABDO Publishing Company online. Web sites about crime-fighting animals are featured on our Book Links page. These links are routinely monitored and updated to provide the most current information available.

www.abdopublishing.com

Index